Sex and the Single Girl

Smart Ways to Care for Your Heart

Ellen Dykas

New
Growth
Press

www.newgrowthpress.com

New Growth Press, Greensboro, NC 27404
www.newgrowthpress.com
Copyright © 2012 by Ellen Dykas.

All Scripture quotations, unless otherwise indicated, are from the *Holy Bible, English Standard Version*® (ESV®), copyright © 2000, 2001 by Crossway Bibles, a division of Good News Publishers. Used by permission. All rights reserved.

Scripture quotations marked NIV are from the *Holy Bible, New International Version*®, NIV®. Copyright © 1973, 1978, 1984 by International Bible Society. Used by permission of Zondervan. All rights reserved.

Cover Design: Faceout Books, faceout.com
Typesetting: Lisa Parnell, lparnell.com

ISBN-13: 978-1-938267-90-1
ISBN-13: 978-1-938267-13-0 (eBook)

Library of Congress Cataloging-in-Publication Data
Dykas, Ellen, 1965–
 Sex and the single girl : smart ways to care for your heart / Ellen Dykas.
   p. cm.
 Includes bibliographical references and index.
 ISBN-13: 978-1-938267-90-1 (alk. paper)
 1. Sex—Religious aspects—Christianity. 2. Single people—Sexual behavior. 3. Single people—Religious life. 4. Christian women—Religious life. 5. Christian women—Sexual behavior. I. Title.
 BT708.D95   2012
 248.8'432—dc23
                                                        2012027948

Printed in Canada

21 20 19 18 17 16 15 14   4 5 6 7 8

Katie waited nervously for Beth to respond. She had just admitted—again—to a weekend of messing around with her boyfriend. Josh was a nice enough guy. He said he loved God and he'd told Katie that he didn't want her to do anything that made her uncomfortable. But being uncomfortable wasn't the problem. She enjoyed their sexual encounters. The emotional and physical rush she experienced had become something she didn't want to live without.

However, because she was a Christian, she wasn't *spiritually* comfortable with what was becoming a big part of their relationship. She had talked with Beth more than once about how she believed that what she was doing was wrong, but deep down she wasn't sure she wanted to give up the sexual part of the relationship. After all, she had stopped masturbating since she'd started dating Josh. That habit felt more shameful than what she did with him. *What's the big deal?* Katie told herself. *It's not like we're having actual "sex"—not really. Beth doesn't understand anyway. She can lie down next to her husband Craig every night and have sex whenever she wants!*

~ ~ ~

Emily and Beth had been close friends since college. They had been in each other's weddings and hung out as married couples until two years ago, when Emily's husband left her and their two kids for another

3

woman. Emily was crushed. Bitterness toward God combined with despair and loneliness to create a wall around her heart.

Beth had continued to check in with her friend and grown increasingly concerned about the "innocent" fun Emily said she was having late at night, in online chat rooms. Sure, she admitted, sometimes the chats turned pretty sexual, but so what? She didn't trust men anymore, certainly not enough to deal with them in person. The online fantasy world seemed safe and harmless in comparison. Beth's heart sank when Emily said, "One thing's for sure: I won't get my heart broken and I won't get pregnant from these guys! When I've had enough, I just log off and drift off to sleep to my own fantasies."

~ ~ ~

When Marissa visited a Thursday morning Bible study, she caught Beth's eye. Marissa seemed confident and strong, yet gentle. When they got together for a walk a week later, Beth was intrigued to hear that Marissa had become a Christian just eight months earlier, after ending a five-year relationship that had become unhealthy and obsessive. In the loneliness that followed, Marissa had talked with a Christian coworker, and for the first time in her life, she trusted in God's love for her. The past months had been a time of freedom from the guilt she had felt over her sexual past. Beth asked Marissa, "How has God comforted you after ending such a long relationship with your boyfriend?"

"Beth," Marissa quietly responded, "I broke up with my *girlfriend* of five years, not a guy. I know that's not cool with a lot of Christians, but since my early twenties, I've only been involved with women. I don't know if I'll ever want to date a man. Is that my only option if I want enjoy myself sexually?"

~ ~ ~

Following Jesus while navigating life, relationships, and sexuality can be tough for single women these days. I know because I'm one of them! Singleness is not a one-size-fits-all category. You may be single for a short time before you marry in your twenties or thirties. You may be single once again—unexpectedly—after divorce or the death of your spouse. You may be single for most or all of your life, by choice or simply because you never met the right person. No matter what the reason for your circumstances, you have to learn how to deal with your sexuality as a single woman. And you have to do so in a social climate that gives little support to the Bible's stance on these issues.

Not that long ago sex outside marriage was not the norm (you or your parents may remember that time). The ideal for a woman, if not for a man (that's another whole story!), was to be a virgin on your wedding night.

Your husband would be your first sexual partner, and most people believed that your goal was to be married to him for life.

Sex Is Everything; Sex Is Nothing

Obviously, a lot has changed. Today society seems to have two gears when it comes to sex: (1) Sex is everything and (2) Sex is nothing. Neither attitude provides much help for a woman who wants her commitment to Christ to be reflected in her sex life.

The people who say sex is everything see sexual expression as fundamental to their identity. This is different from seeing sexuality—your identity as a woman or a man—as a building block for the way you see yourself, interact in relationships, and experience life. To say that sex is everything is to see *having* sex as the most important way to express who you are. For some people it's even more than that—it is a way to *become* yourself. This obviously assigns a lot of meaning to sexual behavior. And interestingly it is most concerned with *you*—not your partner, not your relationship, not your commitment. It's much more about feeling whole, alive, and fulfilled *yourself*. More about that later.

The people who say that sex is nothing don't have such lofty ideas. Their point is that we *are* sexual beings so it's only natural to act on our sexual desires. It's simply who we are; we have a need, a desire, and an interest so why not enjoy it? You don't need to be concerned about commitment or identity or any of that. Lighten up, be smart, be careful, choose wisely, but choose— and enjoy yourself!

Isn't it interesting that whether people assign a lot of meaning to sex or a little, their advice is to go ahead and be sexually active? In contrast, the Bible approaches sex in a very different way, for reasons that reflect a much deeper understanding of how we are made (and by whom) and what we need (and how we get it).

A Better Way to View Sex—From the One Who Made You

Anyone who thinks that God is anti-sex has clearly not read his book. One section, the Song of Songs, is focused entirely on sexual love between a man and woman in the context of marriage, which the Bible depicts as a lifelong union between a husband and wife. It's not simply an allegory for something spiritual, it features the glories and pleasure of sexual love itself. And no one could accuse the Bible of downplaying the significance of sex when you realize that marriage, including the sexual relationship, is said to illustrate Christ's relationship with his church. You can't get much more exalted than that!

At the same time, there are limits to how much meaning God assigns to sex. For one thing, God would never say that you need to have sex to become a whole, fulfilled person, as society does today. Jesus didn't have sex while he was here on earth and this in no way prevented him from being the truest and fullest expression of what it means to be human. Although he didn't have sexual experiences, he was no less a man, no less himself, no less whole. The same goes for many of his followers, like the apostle Paul and millions of other unmarried believers through the centuries who chose to follow the Bible's teaching that sex is reserved for marriage. This meant that they abstained from sex. It may not have been their first choice, but they found meaningful ways to live out their humanness and their purpose for life without sex.

The Bible clearly acknowledges our sexual appetites as part of the good way God created us, but God's Word does not assume that because the appetites are present they must be satisfied. This is because God understands the power of appetites that go unchecked by his standards for their expression. The Bible is extraordinarily candid about the power of sexual attraction and activity. It tells lots of stories and offers lots of counsel about the ways this reality can be used for good and bad.

What "Everyone" Fails to See

It might seem to you like everyone around you accepts our culture's view of sexuality. And maybe they do! But that doesn't mean that this is the right way to think or even what is in your best interests. Our world (and everyone who thinks like this) is a little selective and short-sighted about the "naturalness" of sexual expression. If it's so natural, harmless, and easy, why has increased sexual activity increased our problems with sex and sexual relationships, instead of easing them? Why is "casual" sex so often heartbreaking and demeaning? Why aren't marriages happier sexually and thus more stable overall? Sex is still an area of tremendous relational strife. Why does pornography so often become an addiction requiring more-more-more to provide the same release? It would seem that the naturalness of sex does not flourish as well without commitment and boundaries.

For those who hope that sex will provide the meaning, wholeness, and fulfillment they seek as women, there is disappointment too. When so much of your identity is tied up with a "successful" experience, it is asking a lot of the experience! And it is asking a lot of a partner who is seeking the same thing for himself. The self-absorption and need at the core of the encounter get in the way of pleasure and intimate connection. This is another reason the Bible's perspective on sex reflects so much wisdom about human nature. As a gift from God, sex is neither everything nor nothing! It is a gift to be enjoyed within the confines God intended. It will not bring you life, which means you will not miss out on a fulfilled life if you go without it. But if you treat it as insignificant and casual, you will miss the meaning and beauty it does provide within God's design.

Maybe you can see a little of how these issues are playing out in Katie, Emily, and Marissa's lives. They have all bought into "everyone's" perspectives on sex. But by ignoring God's guidelines, they not only dishonor him, they also work against themselves and against the way sex was designed.

Katie's sexual relationship with Josh fuels her desire to feel cherished, beautiful, and thus *lovable*. But the time they spend sexually is so focused on their own pleasure that they miss opportunities to know, care for, and love each other in many other dimensions that are vital to a good relationship. Additionally Katie hasn't only given herself to Josh sexually, she has also given him her heart and her emotions. Yet Katie doesn't have a commitment from Josh. She has put her heart and soul into a relationship without being sure of Josh and his intentions. Is Katie caring for her heart? Or setting herself up for heartbreak?

After her betrayal, Emily's online chats allow her to arouse a man's interest and enjoy feeling *pursued*.

But her guardedness, self-protection, pain, sadness, anger, and bitterness go unattended. In fact, all those things are reinforced by Emily's decision to relate to men in ways that manipulate them but leave her heart untouched. If the time comes for her to pursue a real "live" relationship with a man, nothing she is doing online will prepare her for it. There will have been no healing, forgiveness, God-restored confidence, love, or anything that would enable her to trust herself to a man's care again. Is Emily really caring for her heart through her online chats?

Marissa's sexual relationships with women and the accompanying emotional attachments made her feel needed and thus *secure*. But they did little to ease the guilt and tension she felt about her involvements even before she became a Christian. Marissa's life took a dramatic turn toward God when she understood that the best way to care for her heart was to trust him for the security and comfort she was hoping to find with her girlfriends.

As appealing as feeling *lovable, pursued,* and *secure* may be, Katie, Emily, and Marissa's experiences show us that these feelings are not enough to give us an identity —no matter what the world tells us! To look for life there reveals a view of self that is shallow and incomplete. There simply is not enough in sex to give us the strength or wholeness we need to be the people God created us to be. But there is enough power in sex to damage some of the most precious things about our hearts.

God's view of sexuality is so different! Sex is valued as a gift, but it is not the thing that gives our lives meaning, beauty, and joy. When we single women rely on Christ's promise to give us our true identity in him, we live as loved, pursued, secure daughters of God now and forever. We grow as women, as sexual beings, and as humans when we follow Jesus, who *loves, pursues,* and *makes us secure* like no one else can.

Jesus Loves, Pursues, and Makes Secure

The love Jesus pours out on us is not sentimental or sexual, but it reaches to the core of our being to define us. It takes us as we are and makes us better. We don't have to pretend or perform to keep his interest. He is committed to us. His love is compassionate when good friends marry and we feel left behind, struggling to trust that his plan is best. When we yearn for emotional and physical closeness with another person, he understands that suffering. If we let him, he knows how to grow us through it. Our companionship with him opens our eyes to loving others in meaningful, fulfilling ways. His love protects us from human counterfeits that talk about love but make no promises. When we trust him, he does not take advantage of it, but uses it to bless us.

When Jesus calls us to the single life, for however long it lasts, it is not intended merely as an exercise in deprivation. Jesus pursues us with a loving purpose: to draw us close and make us women who can demonstrate that the good gifts of marriage and sexual pleasure are, well . . . good (!), but not ultimate. Truthfully, there are a lot of married people who have discovered that sex and marriage are not the ultimate gift, but there is special power and joy when single individuals live that out by faith. When you respond with confidence in Jesus' promise, your dependence on him brings power into your life.

When Jesus promised that he and his Father would make their "home" in those who believed in his words (John 14:23), he was offering a secure and lasting refuge. Marriage and the haven it provides is a good gift people experience on earth, but the haven we have in Jesus never ends and never disappoints. Married people often learn this as they experience the ways their marriages cannot provide a haven. Sometimes this comes in painful ways, as it did for Emily. Marriage and sexual intimacy are gifts that point to the ultimate relationship between Jesus and his followers. He alone remains completely faithful to his commitment to us. That is something we singles can experience fully even now.

These truths of our identity in Christ will never change or fade away. The battle for most of us, however, is to believe them consistently and allow them to sustain us in the challenges we face. What challenges are most difficult for you? Here are some I have observed among single women of all ages and experienced in my own life as a single in my twenties, thirties, and forties.

Sexual Challenges for Single Women

1. Being sexually abstinent is easier for some than for others. Many factors influence how hard or easy it is to go without sex. Some women have a stronger sex drive than others. But God's design is that sex is reserved for marriage, *a lifelong, committed relationship between a man and a woman* (see Genesis 2).

God calls those of us who are single to sexual abstinence. As we depend on his Spirit to live this out, God will make us women who know him as a tender shepherd with good reasons for the calling he has given us.

2. Past sexual experiences can increase present sexual temptation. Women who have experienced sexual touching, intercourse, or orgasm (with others or with themselves) will have a different battle with desires and temptations than women who have not been sexually active. God designed sex to be physically pleasurable so it can still feel good while experienced in sinful ways!

Women who have habitually masturbated have experienced "benefits" that may be hard to give up.

These include sexual pleasure and release and the escape from painful emotions. But these short-term benefits come at a cost—giving away parts of ourselves that were intended to be shared with our potential future husband. We lose the opportunity to give our sexual selves solely to him; we lose the joy of experiencing sexual fulfillment as an overflow of a committed, loving relationship. What is more, we miss out on the ways Jesus wants to meet us, comfort us, care for us, love us, strengthen us, and build our sense of who we are as God's daughters while we obey in this area.

Is sexual experimentation part of your history? Though these losses are real, Jesus never waves an angry finger to shame us when we face past sin. Yet he loves us too much not to warn us that sex's short-term pleasures rob him of honor while stealing joy from us.

3. For some women, physical affection and sexual touch are so closely tied to emotional intimacy that going without seems to equal a lonely, loveless life. More than a few women have sex just to feel an intense emotional connection. They may be hooked on feeling loved, appreciated, or sexy. Katie had the idea that Beth could have "sex (and the emotional connection that goes with it) whenever she wants" because she was married. But no one can have sex whenever they want! Jesus calls us to have a sincere and selfless love for others whether we are single or married.

Katie didn't realize that Beth and Craig had experienced lots of challenge in their quest for intimacy. They each entered marriage with an assortment of fears, expectations, and desires related to their sexual pasts. Like Katie, they'd had to learn (after marriage) how to trust in Jesus, rather than sex or their spouse, to satisfy their souls when life disappointed. When they stopped expecting sex and their spouse to fulfill them and turned instead to Christ to find wholeness, they could then enjoy emotional connection and sexual pleasure with each other. This learning process continued after fifteen years. The security and freedom that comes from an unselfish willingness to serve the other can be learned whether single or married, which was the reason Beth was so concerned about the choices Katie and Josh were making.

4. Dating relationships are deeply impacted by pornography and sexual sin. In August 2006, a survey of churchgoing adults reported that 50 percent of all men and 20 percent of all women describe themselves as addicted to pornography.[1] In March 2005, *Christianity Today* published a study called "Christians and Sex" in *Leadership Journal.* Out of 680 pastors surveyed, 57 percent said that addiction to pornography is the most sexually damaging issue to their congregation.[2]

Certainly, women sin sexually, just as men do. We can seduce and manipulate in ways that dishonor God and our partners. But when so many Christian men struggle with pornography, it is naïve to think that this will not impact our dating relationships with them. Men's involvement with pornography presents a real challenge for women who want sexual integrity in their relationships. Emily's online experimentation was distorting her perspective as well, by encouraging her to view men as a 'product to be consumed', rather than as people made in the image of God and thus worthy of her honor.

God's Design for Sexuality

The bottom line is that our experience of God's good design is broken because of sin. Selfish desires and fearful insecurity are only a few ways our sinful hearts distort what God created. Here is a short summary of what God intended sex to be:

- *It is Jesus-centered.* In God's world, Jesus is central to every aspect of life. We single women can live out sexuality with power and joy when Jesus is the focus of our deepest desires and affections. This does not mean that we deny having sexual or emotional desires, or that we don't struggle at times to be sexually faithful (abstinent), or that we are condemned if we fall. But remember, the primary blessings of the gospel are Jesus himself and his death on our behalf. As we trust him to help us live as he calls us to live and forgive us when we fail, we are living out our faith as sexual beings.

- ***Christian sexuality puts others before me.*** The second of Jesus' two great commands— "Love your neighbor as yourself"—is at the heart of sexuality, no matter what your marital status. It leads us to not sin *against* others sexually. This includes our thought lives, our affections, and such seemingly "private" activities as solo sex and pornography. No sin is truly private! Others are always impacted. I never have the right to honor and love myself more than my neighbor, and this includes the way I express my sexuality. (See 2 Corinthians 5:14–15; Romans 14:7–8.)

- ***Sexuality is concerned with physical, mental, and emotional attachments.*** As God's image bearers, we are created for relationship. Healthy relationships happen as the vertical dimension (between God and us) connects with the horizontal (between us and other people). Our human relationships were never designed to push God aside. They were meant to deepen our love for him as we serve him together. When we depend on a person or relationship for joy and meaning, the Lord is being pushed aside. That is what the Bible calls idolatry.

- *Christian sexuality is not only possible but good in God's design.* Following God in your sexuality as a single is not Plan B. It is not inferior to married sexuality. If that were the case, Jesus himself was *lacking* since he never married or had a sexual relationship. The expression of our sexuality will change if we marry, but that does not mean it is better.

Being faithful to God sexually as a single woman is one of the best ways to prepare for sexual faithfulness in marriage. Faithfulness to one's spouse (in thoughts, affections, and actions) is not easy! The truth is, married or single, sexual integrity requires a radical dependence upon Christ. It means a fight against the flesh, which Paul says was always "right there" with him (Romans 7:21 NIV). The battle will feel intense on some days, easy on others, perhaps pointless on others. But Jesus is with you and promises to make you more and more like him as you trust him with this area of your life (Romans 8:28–29).[3]

What's Your Perspective?

In my head and heart, most of the time I know how good God's design is—both for what it offers and for what it protects me from. But I've also learned how important it is to be aware of the "lens" or perspective I view my life through. Whether it's my sexuality, my friendships, my attitude toward attractive men, my feelings, my disappointments, my trials, my responsibilities, or *whatever* I face, the lens my heart uses will determine my interpretations of those circumstances— and my responses. Here are some that can distort your perspective on sex as a single woman.

Lens #1: Singleness is second best; marriage is my savior.

This lens steers you right toward discontent, *angst*, and what one friend has diagnosed in me: *G.I.G. Disorder*, or the belief that "the Grass Is Greener outside my circumstances." As a married woman, she has a more realistic perspective on matrimony than I do! The problems with thinking that singleness is second best are many. The most serious is the way it looks to marriage to provide things that only Jesus can truly provide.

Being unmarried presents me with blessings and challenges that are different from those of my married friends. Different, but still good! Jesus radically affirmed singleness as a pathway for a person to give him or herself for the kingdom of God (Matthew 19:11–12). Paul taught that the unmarried have a unique opportunity to live a life devoted to Jesus without the "distraction" of marriage and family (1 Corinthians 7:32–35). If you are tempted to say (as I have at times), *But Lord, I'd like to be distracted this way!* I encourage you to read Philippians 4:11–13. The truth is that the kingdom of God is a dynamic reality big enough to make you fully alive and in which single women can fully participate. A sermon by John Piper, "Single in Christ: A Name Better Than Sons and Daughters," is one of the most encouraging and inspiring messages I have heard on singleness.[4]

Lens #2: Sex is my right, and I need it to be secure and complete.

After her divorce, Emily struggled to believe that Jesus was really enough for her soul's well-being. She felt she needed a man's sexual pursuit in order to be okay. She was blind to the ways her choices were selfish and self-protecting, lacking faith and opportunities for healing she needed. She didn't see the ways her online activities increased her neediness, dependence, loneliness, and bitterness—all the things she was trying to avoid. Worst of all, she was cutting herself off from God.

Jesus steers us away from such short-sighted destructive strategies, forgives us when we return to him, and offers us a completely different solution. He says to us, "If anyone would come after me, let [her] deny [her]self and take up [her] cross daily and follow me" (Luke 9:23). Jesus doesn't stop there, though! He also said, "If anyone loves me, [she] will keep my word, and my Father will love [her], and we will come to [her] and make our home with [her]" (John 14:23). Our hearts again become places where we can give and receive love without being controlled by fear because Jesus is at home there.

Lens #3: Feeling pain is death; feeling comfort is life.

When avoiding emotional pain is our ultimate goal, sex and emotionally entangled relationships seem like an easy fix—at least at first. This was what kept Marissa in an emotionally dependent relationship for years. It was messy and smothering, but she could count on her partner's craving for her attention, affection, and touch. Their sexual connection was secondary to their emotional dependence, so it took Marissa years to let go of the comfort it gave her.

Emily and Katie used this lens too, and most people (women and men, single and married) struggle with this to some degree. It results in all kinds of disordered living, especially "disordered worship" or what the Bible calls *idolatry*, when we turn away from Jesus to turn to other things (see Jeremiah 2:11–13).

What we most need as single women is a radical, Jesus-centered lens for all of life. We want to understand who Jesus is, what he offers us, what he calls us to as his followers, and why. We need to learn how to see every aspect of our lives through his Word. As we do, increasingly he gives our hearts what we most need: security, protection, love, forgiveness in our failures, comfort for our heartache, peace in place of fears, unfailing love instead of insecurity, and hope and joy instead of shame. Sex can never give us these things, whether we are single or married. It is a good gift, but it is not the Giver, who freely offers *himself* to us. For those of us who are single, a deeper relationship with Jesus will show us the reasons not to abuse that gift by using it any way we want.

The Best Way to Care for Your Heart

As single women, Jesus ultimately is not calling us to keep rules or lists of "don'ts," answer endless accountability questions, or say no to everything that feels precious to us. God *is* calling us to an ever-deepening relationship with him, enriched as we grow in wisdom through his Word. Here are some ways I am learning to participate in this:

1. Cultivate your relationship with Jesus and with those who love him.

Jesus is the Creator of not only you, but of relationships, sexuality, and all good things (see Colossians 1:16). He forgives us for any sexual sin we've committed. He heals and comforts us when we've been sinned against. And going forward, through his Spirit, Jesus gives us the grace to say no to self-centered desires and to express our faith through loving others rather than seeking to make life all about ourselves.

Jesus knows and loves us individually and specifically. He shepherds each of us with particular help and wisdom. To live life sexually as he intended, we need him to be our personal Savior for our specific struggles. Here is what he offers us as we seek to follow him in the sexual area of our lives.

Jesus

- Gives us himself (John 14:18) through his Spirit and his Word. Staying in the Bible is a need we never outgrow. Beth began a Bible study with Katie, focusing on passages that related to her relationship with Josh. Slowly their relationship became more submitted to God's design, which led them to demonstrate a love for Christ and each other instead of using each other for their own enjoyment.

- Understands and loves us in our temptation (Matthew 26:34–35).
- Gives us our identity: *Mine, Loved, Forgiven, Daughter.* Emily was eventually confronted by several friends about her online world. She realized that while she knew she was a Christian, she did not get what it meant *to belong* to the Lord. As she grew in her confidence that Jesus really cared for her in her loneliness, Emily started experiencing an inner contentment—and a desire to spend time with other believers . . . in person! The time she spent with Christians did not erase her longing for marriage, but that desire no longer controlled her.
- Empowers us to resist and escape temptation (1 Corinthians 10:13–14).
- Gives us sisters and brothers to shepherd us. They are his family and community (and yours!), intended to encourage, teach, counsel, comfort, guide, and love us (Hebrews 3:12–13; 10:24–25). After Marissa told Beth about her homosexuality, the two of them met every month to talk about the Christian life, including what God says about sex, relationships, marriage, and same-sex attraction. God used their relationship to help both women grow in

understanding of how the gospel really is good and practical news for all of us.

• Gives us a calling to be lived out with him. This has everything to do with the way we live out our sexuality. We abstain from certain things but fully participate in others—like his work in this world (Ephesians 2:10; 1 Peter 2:9–10; John 15:5). When I have wrestled with being single and G.I.G. Disorder, it comforts and *compels* me to remember that God has given me gifts and opportunities to serve him *now, today,* as an unmarried person. This doesn't instantly erase my lonely feelings, but embracing God's purposes for me helps me entrust my marital status to him.

2. Determine your convictions about physical affection.

Sexual intercourse is only meant to be experienced within marriage, so if you are single it's unwise to participate in anything that leads to the sexual arousal that God intended to be fulfilled through intercourse. Does that mean a hands-off, no-touch guideline unless you are married? For some singles it *may* mean exactly that! Following Christ requires radical obedience. The key question isn't "How far can I go?" but rather "What limits do I need so that I don't tempt my mind, my body, or the person I'm with?" "How far can I go?" is a question with many gray areas, but the second question helps you think about basic principles that can guide you in answering it.

Singles might think, *But we don't have a sanctioned outlet for our sexual desires. What are we supposed to do?!* This is an excellent question. The answer for us is the same as it is for any Christian battling temptation: we must believe that God will provide a way out of the temptation and the strength to engage the battle daily. Sexual faithfulness or chastity, like many spiritual disciplines, involves abstaining from something that is admittedly natural. Lauren Winner's thoughts here are encouraging.

> . . . the unmarried Christian who practices
> chastity refrains from sex to remember that
> God desires your person, your body, more
> than any man or woman ever will. With all
> aspects of ascetic living, one does not avoid
> or refrain from something for the sake of
> rejecting it, but for the sake of something
> else. In this case, one refrains from sex with
> someone other than one's spouse for the sake
> of union with Christ's Body. That union is
> the fruit of chastity.[5]

What about emotional desires? Do single women also need to be wise about their emotional intimacy with others? Yes, though this is true for married people too. I have found that a top "Jesus replacement" in my life can be emotional comfort and feeling good about *me.* This temptation to wander away from Christ toward what people can give me emotionally has led to some unhealthy attachments with others.

3. Know your areas of temptation and make a plan to deal with them.

The following are some steps that have helped me:

- Remember and rehearse God's promises to you. We easily forget his goodness, love, and provision. Start by talking about what is true about you, the Lord, and life. Your sexuality is one part of you and one aspect of the intimate relationship Jesus is seeking to develop with you as you grow in faith and love for him.
- Ask God to give you a love for him and others that gives you knowledge and insight in this area (Philippians 1:9–11).
- Learn to "put on" Jesus, *nurturing* what leans you toward Christ and *starving* what pulls you toward sin. If you want a healthy body, you'll be honest and specific about what you're eating,

how you exercise, and so on. The same mindset is needed for your spiritual life. For example, how can prayer, Bible study, and time with the Lord become a regular part of your life? Who are some people whose lives reflect a sincere love for God? How can you spend time with them?

- Think also about things that may drag you down. How do the music, movies, and TV shows you enjoy influence your thought life (Romans 13:14; Galatians 6:7–8)? How about social media and other websites? Do you need to put filters on your technology (laptops, iPads, smartphones, DVD players, and so on)? Some things are not sinful in and of themselves, but they may affect you negatively and therefore need to be avoided for a time.

- Know your body. Be aware of your hormonal cycle and the times of the month you are more prone toward sexual arousal. How does your body react to certain visual, tactile, and audio stimuli? What is the best way to honor God in these areas?

- Ask God to show you when certain men, women, or relational dynamics tempt your thoughts and emotions.

- Give others "meddling rights" into your life. Invite friends to ask you the tough questions

(James 5:16; Ephesians 4:15) about how you are doing in this area of your life.

- Be consistent in studying and praying God's Word (Ephesians 6:18).

The "Yes" Behind the "No"

Committing our hearts and our sexuality to Jesus are ways we express our love for him. The supreme reason behind saying *no* to our desires is saying a lifelong *yes* to the Lord. We live setting our "minds on things above, not on things that are on earth. For you have died, and your life is hidden with Christ in God. When Christ who is your life appears, then you also will appear with him in glory" (Colossians 3:2-4). One hundred years from now each of us (most likely!) will be standing before Jesus, seeing him in all his glory. All our tears, temptations, longings, and struggles will be done. May our responses to Jesus *today* deepen our trust that he will carry us into eternity as women whose faith was lived out in the sexual challenges of life.

Endnotes

1. ChristiaNet, Inc., "ChristiaNet Poll Finds that Evangelicals Are Addicted to Porn." *Marketwire*, 7 Aug. 2006, Web. 7 Dec. 2009. http://www.marketwire.com/press-release/Christianet-Inc-703951.html.

2. *Christianity Today*, "Christians & Sex," quoted in "A Few Scary Thoughts..." *SafetyNet Content Filtering, McG Technologies*, Web. 7 Dec. 2009. http://www.mcgtechnologies.net/safetynet/REC/statistics.htm.

3. If you need help and encouragement regarding the what, why, how, and when of God's design for sex, singleness and marriage, check out articles on the website for Harvest USA, www.harvestusa.org, or the online book, *Sex and the Supremacy of Christ*, available for free download at Desiring God Ministries, www.desiringgod.org.

4. Sermon presented by Pastor John Piper, "Single in Christ: A Name Better Than Sons and Daughters," April 29, 2007, Bethlehem Baptist Church, Minneapolis, MN. http://www.desiringgod.org/resource-library/sermons/single-in-christ-a-name-better-than-sons-and-daughters.

5. Lauren Winner, *Real Sex* (Grand Rapids: Brazos Press, 2005), 129.

Simple, Quick, Biblical

Advice on Complicated Counseling Issues
for Pastors, Counselors, and Individuals

MINIBOOK
CATEGORIES

- Personal Change
- Marriage & Parenting
- Medical & Psychiatric Issues
- Women's Issues
- Singles
- Military

USE YOURSELF | GIVE TO A FRIEND | DISPLAY IN YOUR CHURCH OR MINISTRY